FORTE PIANO

Caitlin Coblentz

FORTEPIANO © 2022 Caitlin Coblentz

All rights reserved.

No part of this publication may be reproduced, stored in a retrieval system, or transmitted, in any form or by any means, electronic, mechanical, photocopying, recording or otherwise, without the prior written permission of the presenters.

Caitlin Coblentz asserts the moral right to be identified as author of this work.

Presentation by *BookLeaf Publishing*

Web: www.bookleafpub.com

E-mail: info@bookleafpub.com

ISBN: 978-93-95784-63-4

First edition 2022

For you, and for me, and for our voices.

trauma

my body is a no man's land, the trenches
of my flesh crisscrossed and covered
in barbed wire and shrapnel; land mines
wait for any unwary step or gesture
to send their fury rocketing into the empty sky
to rain down upon the hapless denizens below

i am at war with myself
and i don't know if there is
any kind of victory available to me
except a pyrrhic one

chronic pain

The ghost of it all lives
under my skin,
haunting every nerve
ending, a poltergeist
of pain and not-knowing, leaving
me to wonder if
the exorcism may finally
have taken hold
this time, but knowing that
no ritual can ever
fully banish this spirit
to whence it comes
because I am
from whence it came.

I am its grave
and stone,
I am its sepulchre
and tomb--

I am the home,
and I am haunted.

flying dutchman

And I will wash you away
And I will be washed clean
within the salt of the sea and the whip of the wind.

And only the Moon will know
that I still walk the shores
looking for you

amongst whatever flotsam or jetsam manages to beach itself;

and each time I will pray that the tide brings you back to me
and each time I will pray that we again can slip so quietly and so still
to the bottom of the waters,
sheltered from the crashing waves of the rocky coast;
the rocky coast where I have been shipwrecked and where I walk,
every day praying that among the wreckage

I will find a familiar face,
and I will kiss the life back into your cold lips,
breathe the life back into your eyes
and you will do the same for me.

Pandora's box

someone I love
gave me a box
made of darkness
and called it a gift
but they left, long ago,
and the box is still
in my possession.

I have spent years
trying to change the
darkness in that box
into light, so that I
could finally release it.

(and here is where
I remind myself of Pandora
and her box, a box made
of darkness that was
also called a gift, and
perhaps some gifts
are better left unopened)

anxiety

your inner demons can only
eat what you leave out for them,
so put a lock on the pantry of your soul,
girl, and put those fuckers on a diet.

you're worth more
than life as your own chew toy.

magma

and it bubbles and bubbles and builds
under the surface, below what you cannot see

but frankly honey if you think that
my temper is volatile and frightening and
explosive, then clearly you've never seen a
volcano in action.

why else do you think this planet,
this volcanic-shaky, tectonic-shifty,
fire-in-the-sky and fire-in-the-water planet
is named mother earth?

petrichor

I watch the under
belly of the clouds grow
and become swollen;
filling with wind and ice
and lightning and I find
myself wishing that they
would burst; split open
like ripe fruit and pour
down on us below
the same way I sometimes wish
that I could shatter myself
like rain and, in the process,
become something
clean
and
wholesome
and
new.

PTSD

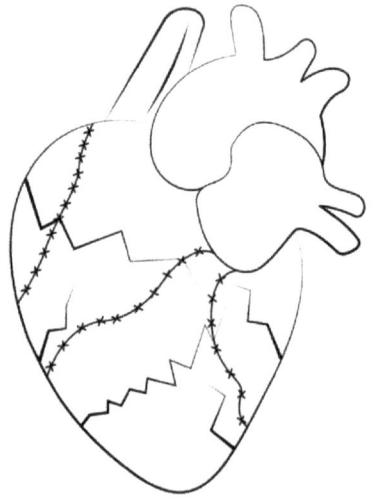

I'm not broken;
I'm just haunted.

I've tried to forget you;
I buried all your memories
out in the backyard,
but the dog keeps digging
up your bones and
bringing them back
into the house.

Perhaps if I plant a garden
where your grave is
supposed to be, then maybe
we'll both finally rest in peace.

recovery mode

the soil sleeps, and
so do I. This hibernation
may be out of season but
it is a sleep all the same.
While birds fly and flowers
bloom, I shall sing to my
weary bones a lullaby,
and offer them a dark
and quiet peace, for a time.

There is no fear in this, only
a sweet ache to be blanketed
by starlight and fresh earth;
it is not a grave for which

I yearn, but rather a garden,
that comes with its cycles
and seasons of rest and
harvest, rest and harvest.

the soil sleeps,
and so do I.

self-love

i used to rebel
by destroying myself
but that's awfully convenient
for this cruel world
so it seems
that my best chance
at revolution now
is to take care
of myself and
preserve myself for
years yet to come
so that i may fill

the cancerous silence
with subtle tendrils of gentleness

song of seasons

Remember me not
in the shades of autumn;
think of me not
in the whites of winter.

But rather,
when all my summer days
are gone, think of me,
instead, as Spring.

Clothe me in the raiment
of new flowers and fresh rain,
of budding trees and
fertile earth.

Imagine me with the
new-born sun,
covered in a garland
of returned stars renewed.

Remember me not
in the shades of autumn;
think of me not
in the whites of winter.

But rather,
when all my summer days
are gone, think of me,
instead, as Spring.

going up?

I am in an elevator
with the lonely expanse
of the distant night sky

despite the close confines
of steel walls and marble floors
there is still room
between the galaxy and I

quiet music plays overhead
from hidden speakers and
in this elevator, the lonely expanse
of the distant night sky reaches
out one nebulous hand to me
and suddenly neither of us
is distant nor lonely anymore

hand in hand, the night and I,
we dance somewhere into
eternity, between the steel walls
and marble floors of that elevator

the hidden speakers play for us
a music that ultimately ends
with the night sky and I

simply spinning madly in
each other's arms as
laughter spills out from us
like the fountain-head of
the sprawling, flooded Milky Way

the doors of the elevator split
open then, unable to contain
the multitude of myself, the night
sky, and the cosmic glow of
our laughter and so we come, like Rumi,
out of nothingness, stumbling and spinning
and scattering stars like dust.

sunrise

I watched the sun
rise across the horizon
of your face — chasing shadows
across the ridge line
of your nose and
the hilltops of your
cheekbones — and then I waited
for your eyes to open
so that I could watch the sun
rise all over again.

sunflowers

it is said that sunflowers
are so called because they
face and follow the sun
as it treks across the sky; and that
when they cannot find the sun,
they face each other, small suns
made of petals and stems.

and so, when I find myself
clouded over and cast in shadow,
like a sunflower looking
for the sun, I turn my soul toward you.

subtlety

i am not subtle.

the ability to create
a screen of discretion
for my expression
is not a skill that i have
any mastery over and quite frankly
it's an almost amusing disaster
whenever i try.

i am not subtle.

my heart is quite clearly not
kept in my chest, behind
the cage of my ribs
where it might be safe
from the whips and winds
of scorn and time, but rather
it is a balloon on a string, tied
to my wrist. in fact,
my heart is many balloons,
each on their own string and
each string tied to any limb
so that when I make even the smallest
movement, my heart shivers
into ecstatic motion, leaping
and dancing around me and
carrying me away to all
kinds of rapture and delight.

i am not subtle.

i cannot be; i am too much
heart and too much
excitement, carried up and
carried away with each new
dancing step I take in this
brave, strange, wonderful new world.

benediction

I think of you
when I wake up.

When I'm still bleary-eyed
and my alarm is sounding,
when the sun itself
is still hidden behind
the darkly blanketed curve
of the horizon, my first thoughts
are of you,
and how much I hope
the new day will love you
as much as I do.

I think of you
when I fall asleep.

When I'm yawning
and my blankets press down,
when the moon
comes out from behind
the silvered clouds, my last thoughts
are of you,
and how much I hope
the long night will bring you

rest and sweet dreams
as much as I wish could.

lover's purgatory

I went to sleep in a
tormented state, wracked
and writhing and feverish,
because the ghost of
your heated body
pressed against mine; the echo of
your tongue and your teeth and
your mouth and your fingertips
haunted my skin and kept me trembling
in a half-life, an afterlife, an eternity
of frustrated wanting because it was
only a ghost, only an echo, only a haunting —
a little death that followed me into
my dreams and back again
into waking, where I would
rather die in truth than let this desire
that possesses me be exorcised

love language

I want to write poems
on your skin with my lips,
dragging out vowels and
biting consonants short, leaving
my words littered across
your torso in the small
starbursts of bruises and
marks; etch myself into
the curves and hollows of
your flesh until I sink down
into your bones; trace the
song of your self across
your shoulders with my tongue

until neither of us will ever
forget how it sounds
hovering in the tremble of my sighs.

I would mouth the creation of odes
across every inch of your flesh,
every phrase and line in praise
of you so even when my words
disappear you might still know
my devotion and adoration.

lunatic

Can I stop off in your bed
tonight? asks the moon
light, pouring through the window,
thick and sticky-sweet like honey.
The night sky is dark
and lonely tonight, not even the stars
are out to keep me company and I
find myself running wild, running
mad, running away

Can I stop off in your bed
tonight? asks the moon
light, puddling on the carpet like
the shadow of footprints.
I'd be more grounded if I
were wrapped in your arms, held
in the close and heavy secret
space between your body
and the sheets; I'd be able to
find myself there.

Can I stop off in your bed
tonight? asks the moon
light, hovering by the door
like a shy child. I find myself chilled

and shivering, and I need your warmth
to bring me to life again.

Come to bed, I tell the moon
light. Come curl up with me, tangle
yourself in the safety of my arms and
my sheets. I'll hold you close and
hold you here, spirit you back
to wherever you last left your soul,
and then I'll bring you home here again
for my bed is also empty
without you here beside me.

third set

Someone,
somewhere,
is playing
a waltz

and I am here,
instead, in stillness
and in silence while
all around me the universe
marks out time as 1 – 2 – 3 –

Someone,
somewhere,
is playing
a waltz

and I am here,
instead, on the edges
of a cosmic dance floor
while all of existence swirls
Around me in a show of
dizzying arrays and bewildering displays
of sound and taste and color.

Someone,
somewhere,
is playing
a waltz

and I am here
to learn to dance.

rest in love

I don't want
to rest in peace
when I die.

I want to rise
from the grave as
the unquiet dead and
laugh uproariously; I want
to sing and shout and
swing from the chandeliers. I
want to dance on tabletops,
my soul free
in a way I'm not sure
that flesh can ever be.

I want to wipe your face
of its tears. I want to pull you
up on the table with me. I want
to gorge myself on your memories
of me, share them between us
like a glass of bubbly wine
passed back and forth until
we both fall over, consumed by giggles.

I don't want
to rest in peace
when I die.

I don't want my death
to be calm or quiet or
somber or grave; I want to be loud!

When I die, I want
to rest in joy,
rest in passion,
rest in delight,
rest in laughter,
rest in kisses,
rest in song,
rest in wonder,
rest in grace —

And if there is,
in fact,
a God,
and if that God is
good and true,
then oh,
God willing,
oh then when I die
I will rest in love.

Printed in the USA
CPSIA information can be obtained
at www.ICGtesting.com
LVHW021413061023
760084LV00102B/1560